Sound of a Leaf

Sound of a Leaf

2018 Seabeck Haiku Getaway Anthology

Carole MacRury
Vicki McCullough
Editors

Haiku Northwest Press

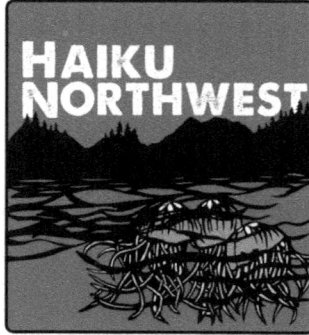

Haiku Northwest Press

Bellevue, Washington

ISBN 978-1-953092-01-4
Copyright © 2020 by Haiku Northwest

This collection of poems commemorates Haiku Northwest's
eleventh annual Seabeck Haiku Getaway, held October 24–27,
2018, at the Seabeck Conference Center in Seabeck, Washington.

Layout and design by Michael Dylan Welch.
Cover photograph by Carole MacRury.

Poems and prose set in 13/20 Garamond Premier Pro.
Headings set in 16/20 Albertus Extra Bold.

www.haikunorthwest.org

Contents

Introduction

The 2018 Seabeck Haiku Getaway was the largest gathering in its eleven-year history, with 82 attendees. For many, this fall getaway to the tiny burg on Washington State's Kitsap Peninsula has the sweet nostalgia of a homecoming and the high spirits of a kindred reunion. For first-timers, rumbling across the wooden bridge to arrive warmly greeted at the Seabeck Conference Center's Historic Inn is often the start of a yearly return. There is a distinct allure to the jam-packed program and the convivial buzz in the communal dining hall, where cheese blintzes with strawberry sauce are an always anticipated Sunday-morning treat. This anthology commemorates our 2018 experience.

Each year has moments unique to that year. Poignantly, Johnny Baranski's daughters Margo Williams and Amy Baranski, and Amy's partner Bob Redmond, led a memorial reading for Johnny, a much-loved Seabeck attendee who died in January 2018. So much of Johnny seemed present throughout the weekend: Bob sharing his bee knowledge—beekeeping, like haiku, is a practice, and in this time of climate change, an activism; at the talent show, where Johnny had crooned a jazz standard, his daughters singing a parodied version of Irving Berlin's "Sisters"; and Amy achieving first place in the annual Seabeck kukai (anonymous haiku contest).

This year's featured guest was Abigail Friedman, perhaps most notably the author of *The Haiku Apprentice: Memoirs of Writing Poetry in Japan* and founder of haiku groups in Québec City and northern Virginia. Abigail reminded us that, as in North America, Japan has had its own haiku "battles" over traditional vs. free forms, season vs. no season word, and 5-7-5 or not. She also explored notions of personal, cultural, and universal haiku and the relative accessibility of each to globally diverse readers.

As anthology editors for 2018, we were delighted to have almost 100 percent participation by attendees. We extend our deepest thanks to all the contributors for trusting us with their poems—it was a pleasure to read them and select our favorites. These selections pointed us to two people who have added to the traditions of the getaway, and we've chosen to recognize Jim Rodriguez and Margaret D. McGee for helping make Seabeck such a reflective and peaceful time:

- Jim Rodriguez has not only treated us to homemade culinary pleasures of the snack sort and regaled us at the talent show with his truck-driving stories, but he has for years provided improvised flute accompaniment for readings, performances, contemplation, or whatever else may be called for. This anthology's title comes from Jim's haiku, and his flute playing is saluted in Susan Constable's lovely poem displayed on the back cover.

- Margaret D. McGee's labyrinth inspired so many poems that we've inserted a subsection of labyrinth haiku, along with some commentary by Margaret. Clearly, this questing tool has had a profound presence at our Seabeck gathering, and we honor Margaret for her guidance in creating it and in walking its path.

We've also included a section on the collaborative poetic form of rengay, with a few words from its inventor, Garry Gay, and a rengay written during the Seabeck gathering by Garry and his first-ever rengay collaborator, Michael Dylan Welch.

We are grateful to Michael for the opportunity to edit this anthology, and we thank the 2018 Seabeck organizers for making this gathering possible. Referencing Wordsworth, may the poems in this anthology bring back memories that "flash upon that inward eye" and "then [your] heart with pleasure fill."

CAROLE MACRURY
VICKI MCCULLOUGH
Editors

Haiku and Senryu

night train
we all think we know
where we're going

John Stevenson

star-filled night
so much space
between us

Gary Evans

autumn leaves
this familiar road
with a new lover

Patrick Gallagher

on the front porch
right where it should be
rocking chair

Dana Grover

Seabeck getaway—
all the lists
I've left behind

Susan M. Callan

I've never been here before
no, wait
I recognise that raindrop

Rosetta McGee

evergreen bling—
poem cards dance
in the autumn breeze

Diane Wallihan

friend to friend
long talks
about short poems

Nancy Bright

the breakfast bell rings
Captain Haiku
still in his robe

John S Green

noisy crows
and haiku poets
flock to breakfast

Arlene Springer

at the haiku meeting
the wood floor planks
short long short

Seren Fargo

haiku workshop
the fir needles we tracked in
point every which way

Margaret D. McGee

dinner bell
    we are already stuffed
with conversation

Christopher Herold

silence at the table
waiting for someone else
to deliver the cutline

Janet Whitney

bookmaking
the sound of cornhusks
in origami folds

Cyndi Lloyd

Indian summer
the new folds of a book spine
binding my words

Margo Williams

big-leaf maple
the entire trail
tiled brown and yellow

C. R. Manley

the oldest person
at the campfire reading—
phone on vibrate

Geoff M. Pope

haiku reading
hearts and minds revealed
in the dappled sun

Laura Quindt

talent show:
the tangled chords
of haiku friends

Barbara Snow

the open window . . .
silent snow, scent of berries,
his voice on the breeze

Shirley Ferris

still air
still trees
still me

Amy Baranski

forest picnic—
I take off my glasses
to see more clearly

Priscilla VanValkenburgh

high in the pine,
storing the fall sunshine
—a squirrel

Aleksandra Monk

I wonder . . .
holes by a sapsucker
for mason bees?

Shelley Baker-Gard

trail marker—
the goldfinch always
two trees ahead

Linda Papanicolaou

birders pause
to identify the blossoms
autumn mist

Victor Ortiz

Morse code
pauses between
sapsucker holes

Deborah P Kolodji

a padlock at the gate yellow aspens

Michael Dylan Welch

windy day
my thoughts swirl
around the campfire

Lynne Jambor

shaped by the wind
an abandoned eagle's nest
high in the dead tree

Rinko

flute song
between one phrase and the next
the sound of rain

Susan Constable

adagio
over the inlet
the moon's shimmer

Terry Ann Carter

early morning—
moon lighting the fog
over Hood Canal

Carole Slesnick

phrase fragments . . .
the glint of sapphire blue
in rough water

Dianne Garcia

a fog rising
through the valley
through the trees
through me

Robert Forsythe

never the same . . .
the sea nor the beach pebbles
now dry in my pocket

Dorothy Avery Matthews

labyrinth
we set down leaves twigs pebbles
to form circles

Ida Freilinger

Labyrinth

In 2018, we built a seven-course classical- or Cretan-style labyrinth at Seabeck. This is an ancient, pre-Christian design found in rock carvings and on coins on various continents.

This was the third time we've made labyrinths at Seabeck. In 2013, we built two double-spiral labyrinths in the open space outside the Colman Center, where we were meeting then. We built the labyrinths from scratch as part of a Friday-morning session, and then walked them together. In 2014, we again built double-spiral labyrinths, this time in the large space outside the Meeting House, where we have met since. A few of us built the labyrinths on Thursday afternoon, and throughout the weekend participants enhanced them with local materials such as leaves, shells, twigs, and branches.

Before the 2018 Getaway, we sent out notices encouraging everyone to bring poems and natural elements for decorating the labyrinth, which was again located outside the Meeting House. On Thursday afternoon, Chandra Bales, Rosetta McGee, and I "drew" the labyrinth in white flour. On Friday morning, I gave a presentation in the Meeting House about the Cretan design and the history of labyrinths, including an exercise in drawing one. After the presentation, we went outside and decorated our labyrinth.

Before lunch, we all walked it together. I introduced the walk by reading the first lines of Matsuo Bashō's *Narrow Road to the Interior*: "The moon and sun are travelers through eternity. Even the years wander on. Whether drifting through life on a boat or climbing toward old age leading a horse, each day is a journey, and the journey itself is home."

MARGARET D. MCGEE

fall labyrinth
taking a long time
to reach the center

Richard Tice

early morning
crows
walk the labyrinth

Terran Campbell

autumn rain
the crows snacking
on our labyrinth

Chandra Bales

nothing sacred—
crows devour
the edible labyrinth

Janet Whitney

labyrinth
a breeze turns over
another leaf

Cyndi Lloyd

falling leaves
the labyrinth becomes . . .
CoMpLiCaTeD

Christopher Herold

autumn leaves
line the twisting path
my mind turns to Chartres

Diane Wallihan

beneath
the turtle shell
war memories

Jacob Salzer

veteran's grave—
the unrelenting sound
of nearby gunshot

Brenda Larsen

drifting leaves on murky water
a frog's head lifts

Ellen Ankenbrock

night walk
   misty
      with wigeon voices

Tanya McDonald

Seabeck—
a lone duck sends a wide ripple
reaching both shores

Diana Saltoon

walking into a web
it's been a long time
since we danced

Richard Tice

after the house fire . . .
how reluctantly I eat
the last heirloom tomato

Kathleen I. Tice

light splatters
through the kitchen screen
smell of rain

Jane Stewart

Seabeck Saturday—
morning gyokuro sends up
steamy tendrils

Suzy Denner

the recipe
for her pumpkin cookies
autumn sunlight

Angela Terry

while no one stirs—
hunter's moon grazing
the red maple

Bob Redmond

dawn
the moon still up
at Seabeck

Carolyn Winkler

we expose
the heart of the matter
madrona

Chandra Bales

we visit graves
on a drizzly afternoon
old man's beard hanging

Angela Naccarato

rain all night long
I keep my hat on
in bed

David Berger

fall rain
rivulets find their way
through fallen leaves

Stephen L. Tack

a woman in black
crosses the meadow
early morning deer

Garry Gay

deep in the woods
I seek without success
the old cemetery

Abigail Friedman

the path home—
I stumble
over shadows

Carole MacRury

late autumn
big raven, your open mouth,
that slight vapor

Melissa Clarke Ward

alpha doe
she lifts her tail
to warn danger

Carmen Sterba

opaque fog
this dream
that is my life

Terran Campbell

scraping off
the mud dauber nest—
shimmering frost

R. J. Swanson

winter scroll—
ninety-nine crows drop
into the foreground

Ann Spiers

shorter days
a mudshark thrashing
in the shallows

Michele Root-Bernstein

no moon—
slow waves
stalk the sand

Lysa Collins

beach shells
the afterlives
of oysters

Michelle Schaefer

over this water
so many times with you—
salt spray in my eye

Connie Hutchison
(for Jack)

ocean shoreline—
waves sweep my path
away

Roy Kindelberger

septic field—
a late-season dragonfly
here then gone

Vicki McCullough

wind gust
the sound of a leaf
stopping

Jim Rodriguez

downpour . . .
the rainbow
in my rearview mirror

Ce Rosenow

Rengay

Michael Dylan Welch and I wrote the first rengay back in August 1992. We were both at a three-day workshop with a number of Japanese renku/renga masters who were touring the United States and teaching Americans how to write renku. By the end of the second day, I was already thinking about what in the form was working for me and what was not. These thoughts about renku had been on my mind for a long time, but they had come to a peak that day—and I came up with the rengay form.

I shared my idea with Michael the next morning before the writing part of the renku workshop was to start. He immediately liked what I shared with him and said, "Let's write one." So, in a small coffee shop in Foster City, California, Michael and I wrote the first rengay, "Deep Winter." The name "rengay" plays with "renga," which is the old word for "renku." I added a "y" to the end, and it became my last name merged with "renga," so therefore, "rengay."

The form spread pretty quickly after Michael published articles about rengay in *Woodnotes* (spring 1994) and in *Frogpond* (autumn 1994). It turned out that many other haiku poets were also eager for a linking form that was shorter than the standard renku—six verses compared to 36 verses—and had, at its center, a thematic element.

I think Western writers wanted to connect with each other in an intimate way. Instead of writing in a large group, they wanted the personal connection that the rengay offered just two or three poets (Michael proposed the slightly altered verse pattern of the latter). Making the rengay a brief, intimate, thematic linking form seems to have met a need no other poetic linking form offered. Now, more than 26 years later, rengay is being written around the world, in many different languages, and by as many as six poets in collaboration.

GARRY GAY

Forgotten

Michael Dylan Welch and Garry Gay

estate sale—
the remains of a silverfish
in the insect book   *Michael*

    on the unswept walkway
    dew-covered caterpillar   *Garry*

vacant lot—
a dozen grasshoppers
ticking in a jar   *Michael*

termite dust
under the back step
rusted nail heads   *Garry*

    a nest of bees
    in the broken mailbox   *Michael*

forgotten swing set
two fireflies
chase each other   *Garry*

Kukai Winners

First Place

broken seashells
picking up the pieces
my sister and I

Amy Baranski

Second Place

labyrinth
facing myself
with each turn

Chandra Bales

Third Place

so like me . . .
this mottled leaf
still a bit green

Carole MacRury

Fourth Place

the stick
deep in the honey jar
autumn dusk

Michelle Schaefer

Fifth Place

kingfisher
his song the length
of the lake

Garry Gay

Sixth Place

morning meditation
the front door's
creaky hinge

Angela Terry

Seventh Place (tie)

dark water
the sudden slick
of a harbor seal's neck

Amy Baranski

afternoon sun—
a maple leaf falls
on the rocking chair

Angela Terry

Eighth Place

aspen leaves
making light
matter

Michele Root-Bernstein

Ninth Place

autumn chill
a headstone in the roots
of a Doug fir

Victor Ortiz

Tenth Place

deep woods . . .
reconnecting
to a lost path

Barbara Snow

Poets and Places

www.ingramcontent.com/pod-product-compliance
Lightning Source LLC
Chambersburg PA
CBHW051706090426
42736CB00013B/2558